No One's Coming to Save You

Navigating Life After Relationship Abuse

Melody C. Gross

CS Publishing

Copyright © 2025 by Melody Gross

All rights reserved.

No portion of this book may be reproduced in any form without written permission from the publisher or author, except as permitted by U.S. copyright law.

This publication is designed to provide accurate and authoritative information in regard to the subject matter covered. It is sold with the understanding that neither the author nor the publisher is engaged in rendering legal, investment, accounting or other professional services. While the publisher and author have used their best efforts in preparing this book, they make no representations or warranties with respect to the accuracy or completeness of the contents of this book and specifically disclaim any implied warranties of merchantability or fitness for a particular purpose. No warranty may be created or extended by sales representatives or written sales materials. The advice and strategies contained herein may not be suitable for your situation. You should consult with a professional when appropriate. Neither the publisher nor the author shall be liable for any loss of profit or any other commercial damages, including but not limited to special, incidental, consequential, personal, or other damages.

Book Cover by Marcus Kiser
Author Photo by Alvin C. Jacobs, Jr.

Contents

Dedication	1
Foreword	2
Author's Note	9
Introduction	14
1. Safety	25
2. Finances	46
3. Family	58
4. Friendship	71
5. Self	79
6. Re·SELF·tion	83
7. Those Who Harm	145
8. Conclusion	149
9. Bonus Chapter	156
Your Questions Answered	170

Acknowledgements	180
Resources	184
About the author	193

To all of the women in my family.

To every survivor who has shared their story with me.

Foreword

I FIRST BECAME AWARE of Melody Gross as a brave domestic violence survivor and leader through one of her diversity and leadership webinars given through her organization, Courageous SHIFT, and then subsequently by following her blooming work in the anti gender based violence advocacy world. I was in awe of her strength, fortitude, and vulnerability as she explained the complexity of domestic violence and its impact on Black women. However, what most impressed me was her ability to deliver innovative solutions through Courageous SHIFT. Solutions not only for the problem that Black women survivors faced after their trauma, but also how various nonprofit organizations and foundations could create and implement policies and services that catered to and specifically uplifted Black women survivors.

As the founder and former executive director of a Black women survivors serving domestic and sexual violence organization located in Washington, DC, The Safe Sisters Circle, Melody's message and mission hit me especially hard. In 2018, I created an organization that provided culturally specific, holistic, and trauma-informed direct legal services, a mental health clinic, and advocacy programs for Black women survivors living in Washington, DC's majority Black Wards 7 and 8. The Safe Sisters Circle was built on my experience in the domestic and sexual violence worlds in both NYC and DC, where I saw how the cultural disconnect between Black women survivors and mainstream providers negatively impacted their Black women clients. Like Melody, I saw the importance of intersectionality (a term coined by the great Kimberlé Crenshaw) when supporting Black women survivors. As such, The Safe Sisters Circle provides services to Black women by

Black women and women of color service providers with a racial and womanist lens that is implemented through its work.

Therefore, *No One's Coming to Save You* hits me equally as hard as when I first discovered Melody, and it further solidifies Melody as an innovative solution maker. Even now as I have transitioned into guiding other Black women leaders in the domestic violence/sexual nonprofit landscape through consultation and the leadership of a nonprofit with a more systematic approach to domestic violence, Court Watch Montgomery- I am still inspired by how practical this book will be first for Black women survivors, and then for providers and advocates who fight on their behalf.

As any good domestic violence provider or advocate knows, it is not up to us to "save" anyone. That's just not a possibility. For survivors to thrive, they must save themselves. Providers only offer the tools to assist them with this. I have always found Black women survivors as intelligent, savvy, and resilient women fighting to better their lives and the lives of their children as whole women with autonomy and agency.

Melody loudly proclaims at the beginning of this book that after facing police ineptness and ineffectiveness, family members' rejection and victim blaming, and society's lack of empathy for Black women's safety: "No one's coming to save you...No one was coming to save me; I would have to save myself." (p.22)

That is what lies in *No One's Coming to Save You*'s brilliance. Its title, *No One Coming to Save You*, alone speaks volumes. As a Black woman survivor herself, Melody explores ways in which survivors can and must "save themselves" and do the work to heal and thrive after their abuse. *No One's Coming to Save You* is a reckoning, a mindset, and most importantly for other Black women survivors, a guidebook on how to self-heal, self-help, and self-empower.

Melody lays out tangible resources for survival after abuse in a model called "re-SELF-tion." She does not merely state the steps of her resource model of re-SELF-tion, but gives examples, affirmations, and practical skills for each area that will allow readers to successfully apply re-SELF-tion in their lives at the end of each chapter.

Lastly, Melody's vulnerability, which I mentioned at the beginning of this Foreword, is weaved throughout the book as she thoughtfully starts *No One's Coming to Save You* by letting other survivors know that their experiences are seen by her and thats what fuels her desire to provide this resource: "Sometimes the path ahead of you is dense with fog. The clouds are low, and visibility is near zero. You can barely see the next step ahead of you. It's scary as hell! But behind you is literal hell." (p. 21).

This book is a necessity as we continue to develop innovative and intuitive ways in our fight against gender-based violence among Black women, written by a Black woman survivor who has done the healing work herself and is now a leader in her field. Black women survivors and their advocates should read this book closely and critically; trust Melody Gross to lead survivors on the path to "save themselves;" and follow the resources that *No One's Coming to Save You* adeptly provides.

Bonus- Melody understands the significant impact of economic empowerment and its correlation to the less talked about but extremely determinative factor of domestic violence: financial abuse. At the end of *No One's Coming to Save You*, Melody dedicates a section to fighting financial abuse and steps towards Black women's financial empowerment (and thus hopefully a form of freedom), led by her colleague, Nadia

Vanderhall.

Alana C. Brown
Executive Director, Court Watch Montgomery
Founder and former Executive Director, The Safe Sisters Circle
Founder and CEO, A Cultured Business, nonprofit consulting services
July 2025, Washington, DC

Author's Note

A special note to family, friends, advocates, colleagues, employers, and anyone who knows someone experiencing relationship abuse.

We are in a time where violence against women, children, gay and trans folks, unhoused, and disabled people is minimized or ignored. Name-calling, aggressive outbursts, grabbing, stalking, humiliating, and controlling behaviors are normalized through television shows, movies, social media videos, and podcasts. We have come to second-guess or outright distrust the victim and immediately believe the perpetrator. We refuse to pass legislation that would protect victims. We are maintaining the status quo at domestic violence agencies that are forcing survivors to choose between the abuse of their partner and the shelter. We have employers who still believe that domestic violence is not their problem, even in the face of opposing statistics and workplace violence incidents. We have limited programs that support perpetrators in changing their behaviors and becoming healthy, loving partners. Where is our humanity? Where is our compassion? When will we realize we are losing family members, friends, clients, and colleagues, and it doesn't have to be that way?

I've been passionate about this work since breaking free in 2016. I didn't know at the time that my fight for healing would lead me to many stages, working with gender-based violence organizations, ready to do the internal work to serve their clients better, and consulting companies in addressing the impact of domestic violence on the workplace. I had no idea during that chaos that the future-me would work on legislation that would address coercive debt for survivors or that I would train managers to recognize and respond to domestic violence in a survivor-centered way. There was no hint that I would publish a guided journal for survivors in 2021 or write this book at the time.

For me, this book is the one I wish someone had slid to me when I was rambling about all my troubles at home. This is the book I wish some of the women in my family had when they were younger. This is the book that I wish all of the Black women who have lost their lives to their partners had access to before that day. This is the book I want every survivor who is criminalized for being the one who survived the abuse to have a chance to read. "No One's Coming to Save You" is the book for anyone who is experiencing relationship abuse.

While this book is directly written to the person experiencing abuse, there are also lessons for you. Read it through the lens of being a supporter. You can't save us. In fact, I suggest you don't try to. It's okay to listen, advocate for supportive legislation, and provide resources when asked, but playing the hero will not work. We need to save ourselves so we can trust our judgment and make decisions without the influence of others.

As I discuss in the book, during the time in the abusive relationship, I was hoping someone would save me. I didn't think I could take the reins, make decisions, or even take the first step towards my survival. Hearing stories from survivors let me know that I wasn't the only one who thought that. But in each story, the result was that these powerful and courageous people put on their capes and had no regrets about doing so.

We needed compassion and empathy from our family, friends, and colleagues. We wanted them to hear us and understand that leaving was difficult because of many real or perceived barriers. We wanted advocates to know that we are overwhelmed and that their patience and cultural sensitivity are appreciated and desired. We wanted our colleagues to realize that our mishaps were not intentional. We wanted our employers to know that we love and need our jobs, that they often gave us the hope to keep fighting for our safety, and that if we could make it stop, we would have done so. We wanted those in our communities to know that we needed their kindness.

All of those attributes guide us to a life we deserve: one free from violence and abuse.

Introduction

GROWING UP, MY DAD refused to buy me most dolls. The majority of them were white with blonde hair and blue eyes and he felt they were unrealistic and didn't represent his Black daughter with nappy hair and brown eyes. Most dolls did not have hair like mine, which is coarse and natural. The toys that came with dolls were traditionally associated with women's roles, such as stay-at-home moms, teachers, and nurses. But my dad always wanted me to think bigger. He did buy me action figures and cars. He likes to tell the story of how whenever he bought me something that needed to be put together, I never read the instructions and figured it out on my own. That is why I love building IKEA furniture now.

My parents instilled in me the importance of being self-sufficient and never relying on anyone to take care of me. My mother was very much for independence and drilled into me never to rely on a man for anything. My aunt told me to always have a stash of money set aside, just in case. My paternal grandmother would say, "Don't ever let a man buy you shoes; he'll take them off your feet as soon as he gets mad." So much so that when my high school boyfriend and I broke up, I gave him back the sneakers he had bought for me a few months before. He looked at me, confused, and said, "Why would I take them back?"For the majority of my life, these beliefs have stayed with me. When I decided to keep my pregnancy, I did so without depending on my child's father to be supportive.

In 2011, when I made the decision to leave New York City, I did so on my own, as I felt it was best for my kiddo and me. Overall, I made decisions and took action based on what I wanted. I handled my responsibilities, despite struggling with housing and financial stability. My mindset has always been, I'll handle it! To those around me, I was confident, secure, ambitious, fun-loving, celebratory, and focused.

By my early thirties, I was tired. I wanted a break. I wanted someone to take care of me for once. I wanted someone to contribute to the household. In 2013, I thought I had that. At the beginning of our relationship, my ex-boyfriend came across as put-together, hardworking, and charismatic. He was friendly and respectful. He shared that he was a born-and-raised Charlottean and worked a blue-collar job. That differed from many of the men I dated, who were creatives, artists, or held other roles that I will not mention. But those relationships also didn't last. When he met me, I was child-free for the summer and learning more about the city. I would go for a run after work and hang out with my friends during the week and weekends. I made friends rather quickly and was a bit of a social butterfly. I also freelanced and provided entertainment public relations services to hip-hop artists and an agency, a big passion of mine at the time.

However, over time, I no longer did those things as often. I spent the majority of my days with my kiddo and him. I didn't have a vehicle, so I often relied on him to take me places, and there were frequently excuses as to why he couldn't or wouldn't. He wanted to spend all his time with me, except when he visited his parents. He truly believed that he should make all of the decisions for the home with little to no input from me. For instance, he determined how the apartment was decorated and where those items were purchased. He learned that being a man and contributing to a household meant he had complete control and dominion over everyone in the home. Throughout the relationship, I tried to resist this notion.

On the other hand, I wanted something long-term and sustainable, so sometimes I would just give in and try to play the role of a stay-at-home wife (with no ring, and still working!). But this came with a significant cost: my sense of self, connections to family and friends, and almost my life. Giving up my autonomy came with emotional, verbal, mental, and sometimes even physical torment and abuse; it also came with financial abuse.

The abuser would sometimes not pay his portion of the bills, borrow money and not pay it back, and even withhold it until I listened to him go on and on about what I was doing wrong in the relationship or with my parenting. I didn't feel like myself anymore. I dressed differently, carried myself with less confidence, and struggled with how I showed up in the world. I would start to regain my ambition, but it would then be pushed out of me, figuratively and sometimes literally. At work, I hid it very well. I was still creative and hardworking, but I was nowhere near the level that I had previously been. I was able to fly under the radar because I was only part-time. Towards the end of the relationship, I imagined someone coming in and saving me from this nightmare.

At the time, I didn't think I could do it myself. By 2016, I had to. I had no choice but to save myself. I couldn't take it anymore. The yelling, arguing, walking on eggshells, uncertainty about his mood for the day, and money struggles in a two-income household became too much. I wasn't clear about what I wanted next, but I knew I no longer wanted to be in this relationship. I told him so, and he did not take it kindly. He wouldn't just walk away. In his eyes, it was my fault our relationship wasn't successful. He took no accountability for his actions, his abuse, or his controlling behavior. Unfortunately, he did not make it easy for me. He stalked me. He harassed me. He told horrible lies to my family, friends, and coworkers. He even pressed charges against me, and I received what's called a "simple assault" charge. To make it clearer, my abuser, who had a record of abuse, was able to convince a magistrate that I assaulted him without any evidence. He was using the legal system to continue to try to control me.

Sometimes, the path ahead of you is dense with fog. The clouds are low, and visibility is near zero. You can barely see the next step ahead of you. It's scary as hell! But behind you is literal hell. I didn't deserve what happened to me during that time. Neither did you. A few things kept me walking through that fog: determination, hope, my kiddo, and ego. Yup, my ego wouldn't allow me to go back this time. Maybe it was more so pride. My pride wouldn't let me return, so he could say, "See, you need me." What my parents taught me started to drown out any opposition. "You have to take care of yourself," my friend said to me after she helped me, and I went back. "No one is coming to save you," she added, pushing me even more.

I had to remind myself of that throughout this journey. When he climbed in my window and the judge denied my protective order... no one was coming to save me.

When the police said, they didn't see evidence of him breaking into my apartment, even though the window screen was on the ground. . .

No one's coming to save you.

When a family member said, "You know how you get."

No one's coming to save you.

When another family member forced me to return, even though it wasn't clear that it was safe to do so...

No one was coming to save me; I would have to save myself.

This book doesn't provide all the answers, and some scenarios may not apply to your situation. I wrote this book to give you even just a glimmer of hope and the desire to strive for more in your life. These are the things I wish someone had shared with me when I first started talking about how bad my relationship was. These are some of the lessons that other survivors have shared with me during our coaching sessions, virtual retreats, or even just chatting on the phone.

Experiencing relationship abuse can take a lot from you, and it impacts many areas of your life. In *No One's Coming to Save You*, I focus on five key areas that I believe are most affected after the relationship ends.

In "Safety," I share tips on rebuilding your sense of emotional and physical safety in a few key places. "Family" focuses on how to rebuild and navigate family dynamics as someone who is recovering from an abusive relationship. In

"Friendships," I share ways to create boundaries and even end friendships that no longer support this healing version of you. We must talk about money, and in "Finances," I share how I overcame being underpaid and unpacked my relationship with it. Throughout the book, affirmations are provided to reinforce your desired outcomes. Lastly, I focus on the most critical yet most heavily impacted area, "Self." I'll share ways to reconnect and reimagine your version of yourself so you can begin not just to survive, but to thrive. To focus on your "Self," you must practice intentional healing. I'll introduce you to my **re·SELF·tion** framework.

In her paper, "Intentional Healing: Exploring the Extended Reaches of Consciousness," social scientist and author Dr. Marilyn Schlitz describes intentional healing as "encompassing a wide spectrum of health-promoting or healing-triggering activities." As it relates to life after abuse, I encourage the survivors who come to me for support to focus on six key areas for intentional healing. I describe intentional healing as an ongoing practice within these targeted areas.

I hope this book inspires you to regain your power and reclaim the resilience that has always been within you. Just for the time being, let your ego and pride take over. Let that be the driving force behind your saying, "No one's coming to save me, so I'm going to save myself!"

Chapter One

Safety

I'VE NEVER REALLY LIVED alone. I got my first apartment when I was pregnant, and my son's dad lived with us. However, my full-time job was cut to part-time when I returned from maternity leave. Eventually, this led to eviction and a return to living with family. For many years after, I lived between family and friends. When I finally got another apartment after two years of living in Charlotte, I was excited but also nervous. It was a two-bedroom, two-bathroom. My son had his own room and bathroom. It even had a fireplace (that I never used)!

I was not making much money, but I knew my son desperately needed stability. I was going to keep this apartment by any means. Looking back, I'm sure this played a role in why I foolishly let him move in after he started having trouble with where he was renting a room. I think a part of me was scared to be in an apartment with just my son and me, plus with my experience with unstable housing, I felt some empathy for him. Unfortunately, that fear of being alone and underpaid led to me not making the best decisions. But hey, you live, and you learn. And I learned the hard way. After a while, I realized that my home wasn't safe *either*.

It wasn't just my physical safety that was a concern during that time; it was also my mental and emotional safety. It was not safe to express my opinions that opposed his. It was unsafe to wear the clothes I wanted or watch a show I enjoyed. I was not safe to sleep when I wanted or for as long as I wanted. Many of those acts caused an argument. Sound familiar?

There always seemed to be a battle, and any so-called peace did not last long. Eventually, something I did was judged, criticized, or ridiculed by him. How dare I think differently from him? What did I look like, questioning him about anything? Why would I challenge him on his hate and homophobia? Why would I wear clothes he didn't pick out for me? It was not safe to be me.

After an abusive relationship ends, the concern for your safety doesn't go away. That is especially true when the person who caused you harm isn't willing to let go. Even if they have, you may still feel a sense of vulnerability, of being exposed, checking your back often, jumping at the slightest sound. All of those reactions are normal. Your body may still be in the height of fight, flight, freeze, or even fawn. For a while, you will experience symptoms of trauma. Symptoms of trauma can look like:

- Insomnia

- Outbursts of anger

- Restless and sleepiness

- Intrusive thoughts

- Anxiousness and sadness

- Headaches and migraines

- Confusion

- Untrusting

- Disassociation

- Agitation and heart racing

When tackling your safety, there are several areas you may want to focus on:

- Home

- Work

- School

- Online

Focusing on your safety can empower you to take back control of your life. While there may be people in your life who will help you, handling your safety is in your hands. Take the lead.

After the abusive relationship ended, I changed my schedule. I didn't have a vehicle then, so sometimes, I would take a later bus than I did in the relationship. I would get off the stop before or after my actual stop. If finances allowed, I would take a ride-share. Sometimes, a coworker would offer to give me a ride. Anything that breaks the routine that the person who harmed you knows about is beneficial.

Home

Home is supposed to be your safe haven. If you've ever experienced being in a relationship with someone who is controlling, manipulative, and dangerous, you know home isn't always safe. It's vital on your resilience journey to create a space at home that's yours and safe. Safety in your home can involve relocating to a new location, temporarily moving in with a loved one, installing extra locks on doors, using internal and external cameras, having two ways to enter and exit your space, or placing objects that can be used to defend yourself in every room. You get to decide.

I didn't move out of the place where my abuse occurred. Honestly, I couldn't afford to pay it, and my rent was relatively cheap at the time. So, I had to take other measures to feel secure. I bought a door stopper for my front and patio doors. I placed my bed in front of the windows to block the way to get inside.

For some time, I had a sofa blocking my patio door. I also kept the lights on throughout the night to see if someone came inside. For some people, that sounds irrational, but for me, it was comforting. I felt like I had a chance to protect myself if he decided to come back and harm me. Here are other ways survivors can create safety in their homes:

- Move out.

- Move to another state with your family.

- Inform people that they must call ahead before visiting.

- Enter a local domestic violence shelter.

- Obtain a gun permit or concealed carry license.

- Participate in the "Address Confidentiality Program," which allows you to have a substitute mailing address with confidential mail-forwarding.

- Change all the locks in your home and car. If you live in an apartment complex, double-check to see if the property requires them to change the locks.

- Have car dealerships reprogram the vehicle's locks.

- Place bars on your doors.

- Invest in a camera and alarm system with views of multiple access points to enhance security.

- Check to see if your apartment is legally obligated to move you to another unit.

- Talk to your neighbors and ask them to let you know if they see anyone on your property or at your door when you aren't home.

Although I have been out of that situation for nearly 10 years, I still take my safety very seriously. You have to decide what safety looks like for you. Take a few minutes to answer the following prompts:

I don't feel safe because…

I will feel safe when…

I need the following to feel safe…

Affirmations

- I am safe and secure.

- I am worthy of a safe environment.

- My home is my safe haven.

Work

If you're employed, you know that if you aren't home, you're at work. We spend a large portion of our time at the workplace. During my experience with abuse, my workplace was a break from the chaos at home. Sometimes. Other times, it was just another place for him to harass and ridicule me. Most of the time, our colleagues are unaware of what we are experiencing outside those doors. However, sometimes the chaos we experience at home also manifests at work.

After I left the abusive relationship, the perpetrator would show up at my job. He did this during the relationship, but I didn't think he would do it afterward. But he did, and not only that, he would talk to my colleagues. He told them I was arrested (I was not.). He told them I abused him (I did not). He told them I was going to jail (that was up in the air for a time). It got to a point where the security guard told him not to come into the building anymore, or he would call the police. Did that stop him? Not really; he would just wait across the street.

Staying safe at work has its obstacles and depends on how transparent you want to be with your employer and how supportive they are. I was lucky to have a supportive employer, but I've also been told stories of how employees have lost their jobs because of domestic violence. For example, when the abuser contacted their employer, the employer blamed them. And sadly, some have lost their lives at their workplaces at the hands of perpetrators of violence.

My experience and that of others is what led me to start my company to provide organizations with the tools and strategies to recognize and respond to an employee experiencing intimate partner violence. Remember, no one's coming to save you, so you must take steps to maintain your safety at work. It doesn't hurt to ask for things; they may say no, but we are used to that, so let's keep going. Creating your safety plan can be an empowering experience. You can:

- Request to be removed from the website's listing.

- Ask for a new email address.

- Request a new laptop.

- Apply for a transfer to a new department or location.

- Change your work hours and passwords

- Request an external VPN.

- Inform the security staff not to allow that person on the premises.

- Have lunch delivered versus picking it up.

- Look up your organization's Domestic Violence Workplace Policy for further support.

- Take different routes home.

- Consider working from a co-working space if you've worked from home.

The reality is we have to work. We need money to survive, so we want to do everything possible to keep our jobs. However, we also deserve safety, especially in our workplaces. Ask yourself:

> Do I feel safe at work? If not, why?

> What do you need to know or have to be safe?

Has your employer supported you in maintaining your safety? If not, is there something that they can do?

What is your safety plan for work?

Affirmations

- My work is meaningful and impactful, and I am worthy of safety there.

Online/Technology

With the increased use of social media came its weaponization by abusers to control other people. To this day, I cannot get rid of an online profile of me that I did not create. It looks to have been made while he and I were together. Luckily, it's not in use, but it's still annoying.

Sometimes, changing your passwords isn't enough. This person knows you well, knows things about you, and can use that information to their benefit. Additionally, they may sometimes use social media to harm you further. For instance, the person I was with used social media to reach out to someone I knew, whom he had met once, to tell her lies about me. He even tried to meet with her to show her "proof" that I wasn't who I said I was." Thankfully, she dismissed him and told him to get help. How embarrassing, right?

Here are some ways you can protect yourself online and from technology abuse:
- Change all passwords.

- Create new profiles using new email addresses and keep them private.

- Use a personal VPN to log into your account.

- Set up Google alerts for your name.

- Block your webcam when not in use.

- Set up two-factor authentication.

- Check where your devices are logged in.

- Only accept friend requests from people you personally know.

- Ensure your location is turned off.

- Post pictures after you've left.

- Change your number. Some phone providers will allow you to change your number if you have a proof of domestic violence such as a police report or protective order.

- If you have to communicate with the abusive person, do so as much as possible via email. This allows for an accurate record that is harder to dispute.

- If you have a smart home it is a good idea to ensure the abusive person no longer has access to it or get a completely new account.

School

During my abusive relationship, I worked within blocks of my kiddo's school. That made it challenging because not only was it easy for my abuser to show up at my job, but it was also easy for him to show up at the school. While embarrassed by it all, I had to take measures to keep us secure. I informed the school about the situation and requested that they remove him as a contact person. They were great and ensured a staff member escorted my kiddo out of the school building every day.

- Each school may have a different process to inform them of a domestic violence situation. Do let them know as soon as possible. Additionally, if you can legally do so (if not hindered by custody agreements), be sure to do the following:

- Remove the person's name from the

emergency contact list.

- Remove the person's name from any school-related documents.

- Discuss with your children's teacher(s) and inform them. Sometimes, they are the last to know. Change how your children are dropped off and picked up at school, if possible.

- Discuss the changes with your children. Let them practice the new routes or answer questions. Involving them in the process makes them feel safe and in control.

Situations may arise, especially when children are involved. The goal is to feel in control and maintain your peace. Not everyone will understand what you're going through at home, work, school, or online, but you must keep moving forward. Your safety is paramount to your healing. Utilize any available tools.

Affirmations

- I deserve to be safe in every area of my life.

- My children deserve to be safe.

- I will do what is within my power to create a safe environment for myself and my children.

- It feels great to provide a safe environment for myself and my children.

Chapter Two

Finances

WHEN I FIRST STARTED dating the man who would abuse me, I was making $20,000 per year working part-time. It wasn't a lot, but it allowed me to secure permanent housing for myself and my kiddo. At the time, my rent was $600 per month, my bus pass cost about $80, and my electric and gas bills averaged $200 per month. What a time! The abuser worked for temp agencies full-time. I'm not sure how much he made. I'm guessing it was more than me. Initially, we agreed to split the bills, with me paying the more significant portion because "your son takes up a room that I am not using." Looking back, that was a *major* red flag.

After the relationship ended, I made $22,000 per year. One of the main reasons I stayed in the relationship longer than I should have was that I thought I couldn't afford to live on my income. However, many times throughout our relationship, he would fail to pay his portion of the bills, and I was left to figure it out on my own. I'd done everything possible to care for myself and my kiddo. When I decided I no longer wanted to be in this relationship, I had to determine what I needed to survive the loss of this supplemental income.

An area that is often impacted the hardest during an abusive relationship is our finances. We live in a world where having money impacts every aspect of our lives. Financial abuse occurs in nearly ninety-nine percent of all domestic violence relationships. During the abuse, you may have experienced the following:

- Forced to work.

- Told to stay home and raise the children.

- Coerced to take out loans.

- Forced or manipulated into not going to school.

- Harassed or stalked while at work.

- Fired from your job due to the abuse.

There are so many ways that relationship abuse hinders our ability to earn a living. After leaving the abusive relationship, I had to repeatedly go to court, which meant I had to take time off from work. I am grateful to have worked at an organization that understood and allowed me to take the time necessary to ensure my safety.

During that period, I wish I had learned more about managing my finances. It's still something I have to consistently work on improving. But I've gotten great advice from financial planner extraordinaire Nadia Vanderhall of Brands and Bands Strategy Group. Nadia has a way of explaining money that leaves her clients feeling empowered, knowledgeable, and capable. I've asked her to share her tips for tackling your finances in a bonus chapter. But first, here is a disclaimer: neither Nadia nor I is giving financial advice. We are just sharing tips. Please be sure to reach out to a professional. Now, don't go telling people that we told you to invest all your money in Bitcoin. These are just suggestions. That's it! Turn to the bonus chapter to read what Nadia says about overcoming financial abuse.

In my desire to overcome the financial burden placed on me during the abusive relationship, I realized I needed to make more money. $22,000 was not going to cut it even in 2016. Here's what I did to earn more money:

- I updated my resume.

- I applied for the Supplemental Nutrition Assistance Program (SNAP) because I needed to feed myself and my son, and I felt no shame in accepting this service.

- Obtained health insurance for us. That alleviated the stress of not being covered for emergencies.

- Consistently applied for new jobs. I loved my job and the people I worked with, but I wasn't making enough money.

- I took stock of all the dope projects I worked on at work, which allowed me to share my wins during job interviews.

- I started side hustling again, utilizing my experience in marketing and communications—anything to earn extra income.

- Borrowed money. Yes, there were plenty of times in the years afterward when I had to borrow money from family and friends. It was annoying, but looking back, it helped me maintain our lives. I have no regrets.

- Learned about negotiating. I wanted to

prepare for what I would do next.

- I requested more work hours and a salary increase. I prepared my points, which included successful campaigns, increased audience engagement, and quality of work. My request was granted. In complete transparency, an interview with a local media outlet, in which I shared my struggles as a single parent in my city, may have influenced their decision. A win is a win!

Between 2023 and 2025, I worked with a local state representative and domestic violence coalition on drafting a Bill that addresses coerced debt. The "North Carolina Economic Abuse Prevention Act" seeks to remedy coerced debt and repair credit reports so victims and survivors have another pathway toward financial freedom. While working on this legislation, survivors shared stories with me about their partners using them to secure cars, credit cards, and more, thereby leaving them with tens of thousands of dollars in debt with little recourse. Even my abuser owes me several hundred dollars in unpaid personal loans. We hope that this Bill supports survivors in relieving themselves of the financial burdens left by financially abusive partners.

But what happens when the abusive person has all of the money? What if they are well-known and highly respected in their community?

Recently, a friend shared with me that his ex-wife controlled their money during his first marriage. She determined how much they spent and what they invested in. They both were in finance, but she made more money at the time than he did. He shared that he would have to ask permission to spend money. She once discovered that he was contributing more money to his retirement plan and confronted him about it. He told her, "You control our finances; this is me also preparing for our future." She did not like that. As he was telling me this story, I stopped him, looked directly at him, and said, "So wait, you were in a financially abusive relationship." He said he was, but didn't realize it at the time. I'm happy to share that he is now engaged to a beautiful woman who believes in partnership in a relationship.

While I was able to access some services, there are groups of survivors who don't or can't because of the power and influence their abuser holds in their communities. I've spoken to women who shared that their abuser uses their money and influence to continue to control them long after the relationship ends or the divorce is settled. Many of these men hold high positions and status within their communities. They are seen as respectable in public, yet they are controlling and manipulative towards their partners in private. Several mothers have told me that their abusers refuse to pay court-ordered child support, not because they don't have it but because they know the mothers need it. The survivors shared with me that their abusers want them to beg for the money. Additionally, the survivors feel even more isolated because exposing their abusers opens them to retaliation and sometimes ridicule from their community. Unfortunately, men with money, power, and privilege can wield this over survivors, leaving them vulnerable and in fear. If this is your scenario, I encourage you to begin to build a new community of trusted friends and family. It may be hard to release the life and community you once had but it will be worth it.

Those experiences and stories are why one of the goals of my nonprofit, the Eva Lee Parker Foundation, is to provide financial support for survivors. We aim to remove the barriers to escaping abuse, and one of the most significant barriers is finances. We have found that sometimes, a survivor just needs a few dollars to get to safety. We've hosted a week-long series of programs to provide Black survivors with the knowledge and skills to begin their new financial journey. However, long-term success requires more substantial financial support. Eventually, we want survivors to come to us, and we can say, "Money is not an issue," and support them in achieving financial freedom and success.

As a survivor, I encourage you to reflect on your current situation and where you would like to be. Ask yourself:

> What could I achieve if I had an extra $500, $1,000, $2,500, $5,000, or $10,000 monthly?

> Can I do something to earn extra money? If so, how can I do it?

What tips did Nadia (See: Bonus Chapter) share that I can implement today, tomorrow, next week, or next month?

If money were no object, what would I want to experience? Note: Dream big!

Affirmations

- I deserve a life free from financial worry.

- I am capable of financially providing for myself and my loved ones.

- Money flows to me consistently, easily, and effortlessly.

Chapter Three

Family

As I mentioned earlier in the book, I did a decent job of hiding my experience with domestic violence. My father, with whom I am very close, was unaware until the end. However, I suspect he had some inkling of this. Things were not great when my sister lived with us for a while, and she did not like how he treated me. When my abuser was stalking me, he also showed up at my sisters' and their mother's home repeatedly. Eventually, my dad called and told him to leave me and his family alone. The abuser said, "No, she has to pay for what she's done," and hung up on him. Now, my dad is no punk, and it took everything for him not to book a plane ticket down to where I lived the same day. However, I encouraged him, as I had been encouraged, to let the legal process take its course.

However, there was a time the year before when I tried to make my parents aware, and they didn't handle it in a way that fostered the support I needed. There was a particular incident when I called my dad, and he said, "Well, you know how your temper is, Melody." I stopped talking with him about the relationship after that. And, when the abuser caused me to sprain my ankle, I called my mom, and she said, "Melody, you know what I went through; you have to leave." I really wanted her to say, "I'll be on the next flight," because at the time, I wanted my mother to help me go through this experience.

The thing is, my parents have their own experiences with domestic violence as children and adults. I realize now that their responses were accurate for their level of understanding, and they may have even been on their own healing journey. I don't fault them.

Domestic violence is complex, and the reality is that they just didn't have the tools to support me in a way that I thought I needed at the time. They couldn't save me.

In a perfect world, your family will understand what you've experienced and support and help you. But we know that just isn't the case. Many aspects of relationship abuse have been normalized and accepted in many families. However, you've decided to say no more. You may even be the cycle-breaker. The decision to end an abusive relationship can be isolating. Navigating your family dynamics can be a challenge. You deserve to be free from all forms of control and violence. Somatic-Based Trauma Therapist Tameka Whittlesey, MSW, LCSW, says, "Abuse can be incredibly isolating, even when you're surrounded by people. It doesn't just happen behind closed doors; it seeps into every part of your life: emotional, spiritual, financial, and relational. It thrives in silence and disconnection.

Whether consciously or not, abusers often disrupt connection because they know healing happens through it. Sometimes that isolation looks like physical distance. Other times, it's more subtle, like emotional gaslighting, spiritual control, financial restriction, or the slow erosion of your instincts and discernment. Reclaiming your life means reclaiming your relationships, starting with who gets access to your energy and presence."

People, including family members, can sometimes project their insecurities, negative beliefs, and unhealthy behaviors and habits onto those around them. You are not obligated to accept hurt just because they are family. Years ago, a friend and I talked about our experiences with family members. He had begun to distance himself from many of them. He told me, "I realize there is a difference between relatives and family. Relatives are those people related to you by blood; family is who you choose." I have some family members who are relatives, and I have some family members who are friends. I get to choose people who are loving, supportive, and kind. I have decided not to keep some relatives in my life because they are harmful and dangerous. You also have a choice. But if you are not ready to make that choice, I encourage you to set boundaries and reflect on the following:

1. Determine what a healthy family relationship looks like for you

2. Create your non-negotiables. These are the things that no family member is allowed to break (e.g., saying things like "It's your fault they hit you").

3. Decide what you are willing to share. No matter how often people ask, you don't have to discuss your experience. You don't owe them your pain, even if they've chosen to help you.

When children are involved, things can be more challenging. If the legal system is involved, it can feel like no one is listening. Let me say something that may make folks uncomfortable: abusive people cannot be engaged, healthy, or supportive parents. Abuse and love cannot ever coexist. It's a cliché but it's true: love doesn't hurt.

North Carolina attorney Theresa Viera works with families and shared her insights. She says, "Due to the lack of safety, stability, and a loving environment, children often become direct or bystander victims in domestic violence situations. To combat these adverse effects on children, there are primarily two routes by which victims can obtain protection for themselves and their children, the domestic violence order of protection and custody court order." She recommends consulting with an attorney to gain a better understanding of your rights.

While we are on the subject of children, I want to invite you to think about how you have replicated the patterns of abuse you experienced. After that abusive relationship ended, I said to myself, "I hate being controlled and feeling oppressed. No one should feel that way, including my child." So, I sought other ways to parent more compassionately, empathetically, healing-centered, and respectfully, because that's what my child deserves. Although it may be considered a cultural norm to hit and yell at our children, we also know that child abuse and neglect have long-term effects on children into adulthood. In a 2003 article in the Society of General Internal Medicine, the authors of "The Long-term Health Outcomes of Childhood Abuse" list a plethora of "somatic symptoms," including:

- Nightmares

- frequent or severe headaches

- pain in the pelvic, genital, or private area

- frequent tiredness

- problems sleeping

- adult depression

- aggression

- hostility

- anger

- fear

- anxiety disorders

- and personality disorders

If you are ready to explore new and healthier parenting methods, you can find resources on parenting websites, Facebook groups for conscious and gentle parenting, and your local library.

Prompts for parenting

> How do I want my children to treat me as an elder? What do I want them to remember me for?

> In what ways am I replicating the harm I experienced to my children?

What steps can I take to become a nonviolent parent? What do I need to stop doing?

Prompts for family

Who are my supportive family members? Who are the unsupportive ones?

What boundaries do I need to maintain with my family?

What steps can I take to engage with my family in a healthy way?

What are the circumstances I no longer want to accept within my family?

Affirmations:

- I am a loving, compassionate, patient, nurturing, respectful, and kind parent to my children.

- My children deserve the healthiest version of me.

- I can recognize and self-regulate my emotions and practice empathy with my children.

- Every day, I am becoming the parent my children need, want, and deserve.

- I am capable of loving my family from a distance.

- I am capable of setting healthy boundaries with my family.

Chapter Four

Friendship

MY FRIENDS, ESPECIALLY THOSE in New York, often were my lifeline. I've lived with them, worked alongside them, and we've achieved significant milestones together. Many of us still talk to each other almost daily. My friendships often consisted of lots of laughing, dancing, long conversations, and fun. At the time of the abusive relationship, I didn't have many friends in Charlotte, just a couple, and our friendships were still new. So, much of what my friends knew about the relationship they didn't witness; instead, they learned through text messages and phone calls. It just wasn't the same and I believe they noticed it. I wasn't the same Melody. Recently, I came across an old email I sent to one of my best friends, providing her with the abuser's contact information, and said, "I don't think anything will happen, but I just think you should have it." Reflecting, that just wasn't true. I subconsciously thought that something could happen, and I wanted someone to know who he was and how to reach him.

Next to family, your friendships are the closest group of people to you. Often, we rely on or expect our friends to "get it." It is disappointing when they don't, and even more heartbreaking when they don't support us. You have choices. You can accept that your friend isn't supportive and keep them at a distance, cut ties, or make an effort to educate them so they better understand. It's totally up to you.

I've been blessed to have friends who get it, but I also know a few of them didn't understand how I got in the position of experiencing relationship abuse. I have always been the "tough friend." I didn't take any mess from anyone and stood up for myself. So, it was challenging for them to see me so vulnerable and not like myself. They shared that they suspected something was up but didn't know what to do. The majority of them don't live in my state. One friend called a hotline when she thought something wasn't right. She said, "I called and told them about how he had physically hurt you and that I thought it was going to be over, but you were back with him. I remember the call vividly because I know this sounds judgey, but I was just so confused and shocked about how this could happen to you. You've always been the one not to take any mess. So I couldn't understand why you went back. The hotline helped me understand the dynamics of domestic violence and told me how to support you. I cried the entire time on the phone, but I hung up knowing how to be there for you and give out resources if you ask for them." Since they didn't turn their backs on me, I chose to keep them in my life.

I have also been told horror stories from survivors whose friends not only ignored them or didn't believe them, but some outright chose the abusive person over the friendship. That can happen a lot when the abusive person develops a friend group or is an influential person in the community. Sadly, it's another tactic to leave the survivor helpless and without support.

Let's say you have a friend who knows you have experienced relationship abuse. They've been asking you what happened for a while, but you've hesitated to say anything and brushed it off. They keep asking, and you finally decide to address it. Here's how that conversation can go so that you feel empowered and able to set clear boundaries:

> Friend: Hey, I saw your ex the other day. What happened between you two? You can tell me; I'm your friend.
>
> You: I appreciate that you are my friend and know you want to be supportive. But I'd prefer not to share my experience. I'd also like not to be told when you do see my ex. Just know it was a challenging period in my life, and I'm still processing it. I hope you can understand and respect my request. I value our friendship.

If you decide to maintain the friendship, here are some ways to do so without being overwhelmed and protect your peace.

- Limit your interactions with them. If you all used to speak on the phone every other day, make it once a week.

- If the topic of your experience comes up, change the subject. Remember, you don't have to talk about it with anyone.

- Remind them about what it means to be friends with you.

- Encourage them to do their research on the impact of intimate partner violence on survivors.

If you decide to end the friendship, you can:
- Explain why you have made that decision and allow them to respond.

- Explain why you chose to block them.

- Block them! No explanation is needed.

- Nurture new friendships that are kind and supportive.

Over time, friendships will evolve as certain situations shape them. You are in a space of intentional healing; therefore, you need friendships to support you fully.

Prompts for Friendship

> What do I need from my friendships during this version of me?

> Who are my friends who are supportive and kind? Who are the ones who aren't?

What are my non-negotiables for my friendships?

Affirmations

- I deserve friendships that are loving, compassionate, supportive, and kind.

- My friendship is reciprocated and appreciated.

Chapter Five

Self

I wish I could confidently tell you that if you work on the other areas of this book, then working on yourself will be easy. I wish I could say, "If you do this for six months, you'll feel better." I can't, and I won't. Working on areas of yourself will be the most challenging and most-impacted area you'll have to address. Remember, this is the area that the abusive person worked to destroy the most. It will take time, but you can reach a point where you can love and trust yourself.

In my experience as a survivor and working with survivors, I have found that six key areas make up the path to intentional healing. As I shared in the introduction, intentional healing is a practice. A practice is something that you incorporate into your daily life to support your growth and development in a particular area, such as healing after abuse.

As I listened to stories from survivors, whether they were actively trying to escape or had left years ago, something stood out to me. Each of them was fighting to reorient towards their true self. Many of them struggled to trust the decisions they had to make, to be able to show themselves compassion and grace, or even know their self-worth. That is all valid when you are just trying to survive. That can be especially challenging when the abusive person is still actively in your life, whether through co-parenting or other reasons.

Before we can repair, we may want to face some truths and beliefs we've told ourselves. There are ideas, feelings, and opinions we tell ourselves that, in all honesty, may no longer serve us. I said to myself that yelling was a normal part of a relationship, or that I needed to prove myself worthy of someone's life and attention continuously. This led me to ignore parts of myself that felt unfulfilled and overburdened.

> What have you told yourself about your role and responsibilities in relationships?
>
>
>
> What beliefs do you hold about intimate relationships?

What ideas of yourself do you find most often conflict with what others think of you?

As a survivor, what new ways do you want to view yourself?

Chapter Six

Re·SELF·tion

NOW THAT YOU ARE free, you can prioritize your needs, wants, and desires. I want to provide you with a resource to refer to when you feel overwhelmed, confused, frustrated, or tired. All of those feelings are valid and can feel like too much to bear. I want to remind you that my suggestions are not a replacement for therapy. Therapy is beautiful and I would not be where I am had I not had the opportunity to attend even just a few sessions. It doesn't hurt to have more support during this time. My goal for this chapter is to provide you with a resource to refer to when you feel overwhelmed, confused, frustrated, or tired.

You are in a period of your life I call **re·SELF·tion**. I define **re·SELF·tion as restoring yourself after experiencing relationship abuse.** After each area, you'll have space to practice re·SELF·tion. But first, let's discuss the six areas that make up the re·SELF·tion period.

> **Self-love**
> **Self-control**
> **Self-worth**
> **Self-discovery**
> **Self-compassion**
> **Self-trust**

Each of these parts of you is interconnected. You can focus on one area, and it may help another. However, I've found that when I gave each of them my attention, I felt better, more secure, and more confident. You are not to blame for the abuse you experienced; however, you are responsible for your healing. The suggestions in this chapter are not to replace the much-needed work of a therapist. It's to complement them. Working on yourself takes a lot of practiced, loving self-talk. You have to become the inner voice you trust and listen to.

One time, after the abusive relationship, someone I know posted on social media that victims of domestic violence did not love themselves. I recall being offended and defensive by the statement and responding to it from a place of hurt. Her post was triggering. Who was she to tell me I didn't have any self-esteem? It sounds like victim blaming to me (insert eye roll). Years later, I realized she wasn't wrong. I didn't love myself. I didn't value myself. I didn't know my self-worth. And guess what? That is okay. Now, it's up to me to love myself so much that I don't ignore the red flags, question the yellow flags, and accept the green flags.

Self-Love

"Do not live someone else's life and someone else's idea of what womanhood is. Womanhood is you. Womanhood is everything that's inside of you."

– Viola Davis

There are parts of me I didn't love for a very, very, very long time. For most of my life until my mid-thirties, I had issues with my body. I felt I was too skinny for a while. I have an overbite, and my hair is nappy. I know because of my internal thoughts about myself, I settled for mediocre ass relationships.

During the abusive relationship, he would go from complimenting my features to insulting me. Shortly before I met him, I started to embrace the natural state of my hair (no straightening). Initially, he liked that I was natural. However, my natural hair required time to maintain, which meant time away from him and his needs.

The thing that people who knew me before this relationship noticed was the change in my wardrobe. I was usually seen as the stylish one, and I always wore heels. However, he preferred more subdued attire, so I rarely wore heels, usually only for special occasions. He could easily shift how I dressed due to all my internalized insecurities. I didn't love myself. I felt like something was wrong with me, and I needed to be fixed. Plus, society already stresses how unpretty and unworthy Black girls and women are, and his behavior reinforced that for me.

As much as my parents told me how pretty I was since I was little, the external reminders held more influence. The name-calling I endured during the relationship magnified the self-love I lacked. At a certain point, things fluctuated, and I had my a-ha moment. I began to understand that my ex-boyfriend's insults towards me weren't about me.

It was all about him and his insecurities. Later, when he said negative things about me, I told him he was projecting his feelings onto me. It became clear his words were a reflection of his issues and insecurities. After every negative thing he said about me, I practiced saying something positive aloud in front of him or silently to myself. Sometimes, I would look in the mirror and say, "I am pretty. I am beautiful. My hair is gorgeous. My body is banging. I'm the shit!" These small acts of resistance greatly helped me. I didn't realize at the time that I was getting back to myself.

You hear it constantly, "practice self-love," or "love yourself." That is especially hard when, for some time, someone is telling you otherwise and making you feel unlovable. I won't lie to you; this will be the most challenging area to focus on. Inner voices are powerful. When you were a child, that inner voice was a caregiver. In an abusive relationship, that inner voice is more than likely the person hurting you. A part of practicing self-love is ensuring that your inner voice is *yours* and *yours alone*. I say practice because it takes time and repetition. It'll take trial and error.

There is no quick fix to loving yourself. It took time to unlove yourself at the hands of the abuser, and it'll take time to love yourself again. Self-love after an abusive relationship can look like:

- Setting boundaries and standards for yourself.
- Prioritizing your needs over others'.
- Listening to your body.
- Going to a therapist.
- Reconnecting with your spiritual practice.
- Learning about healthy relationships.
- Wearing clothes that make you feel good.
- Getting your finances in order.
- Looking in the mirror and practicing self-talk.

Re·SELF·tion

State

Describe what it will feel like to love yourself.

What does it feel like when you aren't practicing self-love?

Act

What does self-love look like in action? What steps can you take to practice self-love daily, weekly, or monthly?

How will you respond when you aren't practicing self-love?

What type of boundaries will you set for yourself?

Process

What areas of your life do you need to practice self-love, and how will you do so? (e.g., family, friends, partners, etc.)

Who in your life practices self-love well, and what can you learn from them?

Affirmation

- I love myself as I am and as I will be.

- I love {insert body part}.

- Each day, I am learning how to love myself more and more.

Self-control

"It's not the load that breaks you down, it's the way you carry it."

— Lena Horne

After the end of an abusive relationship, we may experience loneliness. That feeling can influence us to seek comfort from someone else. Sometimes, that person is the one who harmed us. When we practice self-control, we acknowledge our feelings and emotions but refrain from acting on them if they are unhealthy or cause us more pain.

The time right before I left the abusive person, I was back in contact with someone I dated on and off for years. While I had a great time with him, he never gave me the full commitment I desired. I disclosed what I was experiencing, and he was very supportive. In a way that at the time I didn't understand, he unknowingly pushed me to get out of the abusive relationship. We had reached 10 years of knowing each other, and I hoped this milestone would improve things. After I broke free, we started dating, and although it was a long-distance relationship, things were going great. We would FaceTime and visit each other. But then he disappeared, and I didn't hear from him for weeks. That was always a thing throughout the years. Somehow, I thought this time would be different because it felt different. I was angry and hurt, and when we finally spoke, he was not sympathetic and implied I was overreacting. It was over.

What I realized during my healing process was that I was in no way ready to be in a relationship, even if it was with someone I had known since my early twenties. I realized I saw the person as safe because my abuser was not. I came to understand that I wanted this person to save me. I wanted him to get me, protect me, and take care of me. I was sad, angry, and frustrated when that didn't happen. But then I came to realize what my homegirl had said to me after I went back to the abuser, "No one is coming to save you, Melody!"

I had to learn self-control because I didn't want my impulses, emotions, and negative thoughts to influence my decisions in a harmful way. Having self-control can look like:

- Taking a few breaths before responding to your child.

- Not responding to an upsetting text.

- Not raising your voice in anger.

- Not having sex with someone just because you're lonely.

- Not cursing or lashing out at your colleague or supervisor.

- Knowing when to walk away or diffuse a situation.

To practice self-control, you must be aware of your triggers or symptoms of trauma. Due to your experience in an abusive relationship, your responses to situations and interactions with others can be complex and confusing. Knowing the emotions and feelings that come up for you will enable you to pause and respond from a place of healing and balance. This is not an exhaustive list of triggers and symptoms of trauma, but it is a place to start. The Mayo Clinic provides excellent information on post-traumatic stress disorder, including its symptoms, causes, and responses. You can find the link to this information in the appendix. Remember to seek professional support for any mental health needs. This section is not to diagnose you but to provide you with information.

Intrusive memories

- Recurrent, unwanted, distressing memories of the traumatic event.

- Reliving the traumatic event as if it were

happening again (flashbacks).

- Upsetting dreams or nightmares about the traumatic event.

- Severe emotional distress or physical reactions to something that reminds you of the traumatic event.

Negative Changes in Thinking and Mood

- Negative thoughts about yourself, other people, or the world.

- Ongoing negative emotions of fear, blame, guilt, anger, or shame.

- Memory problems, including not remembering important aspects of a traumatic event.

- Feeling detached from family and friends.

- Losing interest in activities you once enjoyed.

- Having a hard time feeling positive emotions.

- Feeling emotionally numb.

Changes in Physical and Emotional Reactions
- Being easily startled or frightened.
- Always being on guard for danger.
- Self-destructive behavior, such as drinking too much or driving too fast.
- Trouble sleeping.
- Trouble concentrating.
- Irritability, angry outbursts, or aggressive behavior.
- Physical reactions include sweating, rapid breathing, a fast heartbeat, or shaking.

When you have an awareness of your triggers and symptoms of trauma, you can take steps to reduce the negative impact and practice self-control. It's not easy, but it's worth it. You owe it to yourself to give yourself ample opportunities to heal and overcome the trauma you experienced. Having self-control benefits not only you but also those around you.

Re·SELF·tion

State

Describe what it will feel like to have self-control when you are lonely, angry, and frustrated.

What does it feel like when you aren't practicing self-control?

Act

What does self-control look like in action? What steps can you take to practice self-control daily, weekly, or monthly?

How will you respond when you aren't practicing self-control?

What type of boundaries will you set for yourself?

In what situations do you find yourself unable to control yourself? What occurs when you don't? How would I like to manage these situations next time?

Process

What areas of your life do you need to practice self-control, and how will you do so? (e.g., family, friends, children, partners, etc.)

Who around you practices self-control well, and what can you learn from them?

What triggers and symptoms of trauma have you noticed within yourself? Trigger examples can include loud noises, specific places, anniversaries, celebrity stories, and other similar events. Some of the symptoms can be emotional detachment, flashbacks, and intrusive thoughts, among others.

What tools and techniques will you use to practice improved self-control?

Affirmation

- My self-control is my responsibility, and I will do my best to maintain it.

- I recognize my symptoms of trauma, and I will continue to heal.

- While I may be alone, I am not lonely. I am surrounded by those who love and respect me.

Self-worth

"Deal with yourself as an individual worthy of respect, and make everyone else deal with you the same way."

– Nikki Giovanni

You are worthy! You are worthy of love, compassion, tenderness, care, grace, freedom, financial stability, peace, safe sex, security, support, and all the things in between. Someone has probably told you that you aren't worthy. They are ashy liars; don't listen to them. When we work on our self-worth, we tell ourselves we are valuable, deserve it all, and bring beauty to the world. *We are beauty*. We deserve a love that is free from hurt, pain, and violence.

Reflecting then, I feel like a shift occurred on New Year's Day in 2016. It's like even though the reality was I was still physically in this abusive relationship,

I was also mentally and emotionally checked out. I recall that day, my kiddo and I were in the living room watching the countdown and taking pictures. He was in the bedroom on his phone. And I remember just not caring. I didn't care to check on him or ask him to join us. I wasn't wondering about what he was doing. At that moment, I felt peace with him not being around. Even when I looked at old text messages from that time, I could see I just didn't care anymore and just wanted him to leave my apartment and for the relationship to end. I slowly began to understand that I was worthy of someone who engaged in family activities and didn't use the silent treatment to manipulate me into appeasing them. I was regaining my self-worth.

Another area of my life that was impacted by the abusive relationship and my self-worth was my work and, in turn, my pay. As I mentioned in the finances chapter, I was not getting paid what I was worth. I had to learn that I was worthy of a salary that supported myself and my child, allowing me to thrive. I also deserved to work at an organization that valued my work and paid me accordingly. At another organization, I was there for less than a year when I remembered my values and standards of self-worth. While there is a lot of privilege in the decision I made to quit my job without another one, I have no regrets because I was not being valued or respected. I was being oppressed, things that I vowed after the abusive relationship to never experience again.

When you decide to leave an abusive relationship, you are showing your self-worth. When you choose not to go back, even when they beg you to, you are saying, "I am worthy of something different," which prioritizes your self-worth. Here are other examples of showing your self-worth:

- Asking for a raise.

- Going after a promotion.

- Applying to higher-paying jobs.

- Going back to school.

- Studying a trade.

- Applying for a restraining order.

- Renewing a protective order.

- Not sleeping with someone just because they are accessible or you feel lonely.

- Advocating for yourself.

- Asking for help and support.

- Saying no.

Those examples tell your subconscious, "I am worthy of more, and I won't settle for less."

Re·SELF·tion

State

Describe what it will feel like to know your self-worth.

What does it feel like when you aren't practicing self-worth?

Act

What am I worthy of? Think about small and big things that positively influence your self-worth. (e.g., I will stop calling myself stupid; I am not stupid; I am healing and learning).

What does self-worth look like in action? What steps can you take to practice self-worth daily, weekly, or monthly?

How will you respond when you aren't showing your self-worth?

What type of boundaries will you set for yourself?

Process

What areas of your life do you need to practice self-worth, and how will you do so? (e.g., family, friends, partners, etc.)

Who in your life practices self-worth well, and what can you learn from them?

Affirmation

- I am worthy.

- I am worthy of caring, respectful, loving, and healthy relationships.

- My self-worth is my responsibility, and I will practice it daily.

Self-discovery

"Helped are those who are content to be themselves; they will never lack mystery in their lives, and the joys of self-discovery will be constant."

– Alice Walker

Who are you? Outside of the titles, labels, and responsibilities, who are you? Tell me what your interests are. Who you be with? Things that make you smile. *wink*

During that period of life, if someone had asked me those questions, I either could not answer, didn't have a fleshed-out response, or lied. I mean, I enjoyed collecting crystals and learning about their properties and uses. However, I honestly didn't know who I was outside of being a mother, girlfriend, communications and marketing associate, friend, daughter, or sibling—none of which I did particularly well if I'm being honest.

When you're in an abusive relationship, you don't have the time, mental or emotional capacity, or even permission, to discover who you are. You are being conditioned to be who they want you to be for *them*. And, even that is ever-changing. The abusive person I was with wanted me to be more like his mother (e.g., cook, clean, quiet, don't complain). Another part was that he wanted me to be submissive and docile. The other part was up in the air, depending on his mood.

During our time together, I discovered Reiki and explored different forms of African spirituality. He was supposed to be on the journey with me since we both found Christianity not to align with our values (or so I thought). But all it led to was wild conspiracy theories, problematic Black faux-intellectuals, harmful wife rhetoric, and being told I lacked obedience and needed to be more submissive. None of those things were about building a healthy relationship or discovering who I am. Instead, they were about how he would get me to only listen to him, do what he said, and be who he wanted me to be on any given day. What he wanted me to discover was that I was nothing without him. But what I eventually realized is that I am everything without him.

   I am love
   I am loved
   I am powerful
   I am protected
   I am a disruptor
   I am a nap lover
   I am funny
   I am fun
   I am intelligent
   I am abundant
   I am free
   I am compassionate
   I am a master manifestor
   I am everything I need, want, and desire

I rediscovered that I love to dance, laugh, and sing. I also love the arts, including attending performances and art exhibitions. I love doing touristy things. I love Black culture and joy. One of my favorite hobbies is decorating for Christmas. As a recovering Grinch, my family and friends are often shocked each year by how much I spend on holiday decorations, from creating my centerpieces to buying pajamas that match that year's color scheme. I love finding out new things about myself.

As you can see, none of what I mentioned concerns other people, my career, family, or partner. It's all about me, and I love that. I have those attributes regardless of who I am with or where I work. Getting here was not an easy feat. I am still on the journey of self-discovery. In my guided journal, *Reclaim Your Resilience,* I list hobbies and activities you may have enjoyed before the relationship or ones you want to try now. And that's the thing: you'll have to try new things even when you're scared, anxious, or unsure. It's a part of the growth journey.

In the fall of 2020, my partner at the time invited me to go backpack camping with his friend and girlfriend. Until that point, I'd never been camping. I didn't even know I needed to have a special backpack. We had to hike three miles to the campsite. That day, I learned how to put up a tent and start a fire. It was great! It rained that night, and it was still a beautiful experience. I discovered that I enjoy camping and that being in nature makes me smile.

Re·SELF·tion

State

Describe what it will feel like to discover things about yourself.

Act

What does self-discovery look like in action? What steps can you take to discover new things about yourself?

Process

When you discover something new about yourself, how will you celebrate? How will you keep track of the things you discover?

Affirmation

- Each day, I am open to learning more about myself.

- I welcome this journey of self-discovery.

Self-compassion

"We must reject not only the stereotypes that others hold of us, but also the stereotypes that we hold of ourselves."

– Shirley Chisolm

As humans, we are way too hard on ourselves. We are hypercritical of so much of what we do or say. I genuinely believe that we often lack compassion for one another, especially for ourselves. First, we must practice self-compassion before we can extend it to others. I was incredibly hard on myself after the abusive relationship.

I'm going to be transparent with you. This was the most challenging chapter to write. When I reflect on my experience, I'm not sure if I showed myself as much compassion as I could have. For at least three years after I left the abusive relationship, I think even subconsciously, I still blamed myself. I would constantly ask myself things like, "Why did I let him do this to me?" "How did I get here?" "What's wrong with me?" and "Why did I ignore the red flags?" Why. Why. Why. Are those questions helpful? Most likely, they are not. Are there things I would've done differently? Absolutely. But what does beating myself up do now? Those questions were not helpful and left me in a space of continuous self-doubt and victimhood. Plus, that is the state of mind the abusive person wants us in--the constant state of self-blame.

One day, rather unceremoniously, I realized I was being too hard on myself, and the sense of self-blame wasn't beneficial to my healing. I decided to show myself as much compassion as possible; I no longer wanted to sit with the feeling of guilt. Most of the guilt I had was because of what my kiddo endured. Witnessing the arguing, tears, and aftermath of physical fights still makes my chest tight. But with self-compassion, I don't have to internalize that pain to the point of being immobilized.

What if instead, I embraced how researcher and author, Dr. Kristie Neff defines self-compassion in her 2023 journal article "Self-Compassion: Theory, Method, Research, and Intervention," as "being kind to oneself when confronting personal inadequacies or situational difficulties, framing the imperfection of life in terms of common humanity, and being mindful of negative emotions so that one neither suppresses nor ruminates on them." The reality is that I was not being kind or empathetic to myself. Something had to change. I wanted and deserved to be whole. From that point of awareness, I took steps to practice self-compassion. I started to reframe the harsh questions I was asking myself into more compassionate ones.

> Instead of: How did I get here?
> I would say: I took a courageous chance at love, and that's okay
>
> Instead of: What's wrong with me?
> I would say: Nothing. The abuse is not my fault.
>
> Instead of: Why did I ignore the red flags?
> I would say: I wanted to see the best in the person.
>
> Instead of: I'm unlovable.
> I would say: Lies. I am worthy of love in all ways.

Practicing self-compassion means discovering different ways of thinking, showing up for yourself, learning new supportive tools, and creating a new inner voice. Giving yourself grace, especially immediately after an abusive relationship, is vital to your intentional healing. We have experienced something that has forever changed us, but that doesn't mean we have to be unkind to ourselves.

Re·SELF·tion

> ### *State*
>
> Describe what it will feel like to talk to yourself nicely.

Describe what it will feel like to show yourself compassion.

Act

What does self-compassion look like in action? What steps can you take to practice more self-compassion?

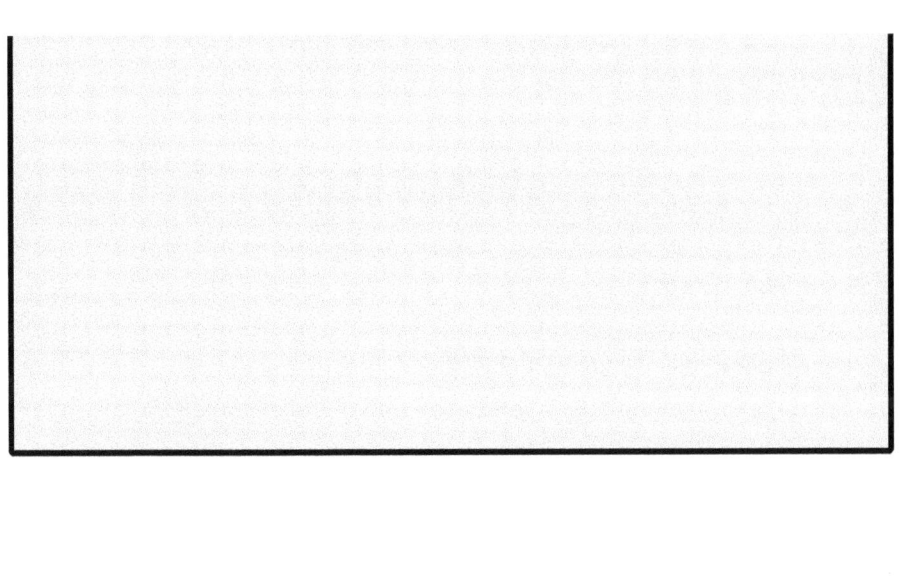

Process

When you're having a challenging moment, how will you practice self-compassion? What tools will you use?

Affirmation

- I am allowed to be kind to myself.

- When challenges occur, I can still be kind and empathetic to myself.

Self-trust

"You've just got to follow your own path. You have to trust your heart and you have to listen to the warnings."

– Chaka Khan

When the infamous year of 2020 came around, I had been speaking about and sharing my story of domestic violence for more than three years. Folks who were currently experiencing and had previously experienced relationship abuse would reach out to me sometimes for advice and guidance, or just to speak to someone who understands what they went through. I am bold and unapologetic about my experience and thoughts on intimate partner violence. I am not ashamed. Shame has no place in healing. I wanted other survivors to experience the same, even if it's just with themselves. I wanted them to know they can trust themselves.

One night in January 2020, I was lying in my bed just thinking about what's next. The speaking engagements were a significant step, but I wanted to do more intentional work with survivors. I lay there looking up at my puke-white popcorn ceiling and said to myself, "What's next? What do I need to do to support survivors better?" And, I went to sleep. At three in the morning, I got my answers care of the sounds of some damn raccoons. My apartment at the time was basic and outdated. It was built in the 70s, and it showed. For months, I had been complaining to my management office about the presence of raccoons in my ceiling. Yes, you heard me right. Raccoons had crawled into my ceiling and decided to live there, and the two of them would fight if one came into the other's space.

So, when I was startled awake to their screeching, I was annoyed. I couldn't get back to sleep, so I opened my journal to start writing. Then it came to me. *Coaching*. Becoming a coach was my next step in supporting survivors. I had previously worked with coaches, primarily for career and business development. Some left much to be desired. Some were calling themselves coaches when, in reality, they were consultants.

Fast forward a few weeks, and I sat on a panel discussing marketing. Afterwards, I met a woman who was interested in working with me to market her business. I told her, "I'm doing marketing now, but I want to become a coach." She said, "Funny enough, I am a coach and I train coaches." What are the odds? In Early March, I started her program, and it was a wonderful experience. I learned a great deal and felt better equipped to support survivors.

What I love about coaching is that it truly puts the control and power back into the hands of the coachee. And that's what I want for survivors because the abusive person stripped it away from us. The tools I learned in the training have become invaluable to me and my personal and professional life.

This experience taught me that I can trust myself. I can trust my inner voice and intuition, knowing that I am making the best decisions for myself. It empowered me to realize that I am the expert on myself, a concept that coaching reinforces. You *are* the expert of your life. You can trust that you are making the best decisions based on the tools you have. While I eventually want you to reach the point of trusting others, the priority is to learn how to trust yourself. You know yourself better than anyone else. Think about the decisions that were often made by someone else. What would you have done differently?

Here are some other circumstances when I've practiced self-trust:

- Deciding on the type of school my kiddo

attended.

- What to wear.

- When to end a relationship/friendship.

- When to walk away from a conversation that is unhealthy.

- When to set a boundary.

- When to ask for help.

- Who to ask for help.

- When I was ready to start dating again.

- When to advocate for myself.

- Taking time to weigh the pros and cons of a decision.

Self-trust is a building block to so many other relationships and dynamics you'll experience during your life after abuse. Self-trust, at its core, is about reclaiming the power and control that someone else had over you. That is the person you want to be independent of, because they are using your lack of self-trust and distorting your sense of self to control you. And, we don't want to be controlled, right?! Build trust in yourself, even if it's a little step at a time.

Re·SELF·tion

State

Describe what it will feel like to trust yourself. Will you feel secure, confident, or capable?

Describe what it will feel like to make your own decisions. Choose one decision that is your own.

Act

What does self-trust look like in action?

What steps can you take to practice more self-trust? Try going one day, week, or month without asking anyone's advice.

Process

When you're having a challenging moment or need to make a difficult decision, how will you actualize self-trust? What tools will you use?

Affirmation

- I trust myself.

- When hard decisions need to be made, I trust I have the tools to respond accordingly.

- I am learning to trust myself each day.

Chapter Seven

Those Who Harm

Before I conclude this book, let me spend a very brief moment writing about perpetrators of relationship abuse. Y'all…

They will not change unless they make the conscious and active decision to do so and seek out the tools to change their behaviors; plus, change can't take place while still actively engaged in harming someone. Those who abuse have to *choose* to want to be different. I'm sure you've been told by them the myriad of reasons why they do what they do, say those things, or just outright deny the abuse occurred.

I believe in redemption. I couldn't do this work if I didn't. But, and I mean this with all sincerity:

> Their redemption isn't your problem.
> Their redemption isn't up to you.
> Their past trauma isn't for you to heal.
> You can't fix them.

Your empathy for what they've been through does not mean you have to endure how they act as a result of that.

You can't, and I repeat, can't, save them.

If the person being abusive is serious about changing, they will do the work independently. They don't need you to research programs, make appointments, or prioritize their feelings over your safety. They don't need you! Decenter them. Period! Search engines, cell phones, and libraries are available to everyone. Let them figure it out. Let them save themselves. Focus on you. Save yourself!

Prompts

1. What would happen if you focused more on your healing and less on the person hurting you?

2. What happens when you pour our energy and time into the person causing you harm? What, if anything, changes?

3. Who would benefit from you addressing your healing and trauma to become the version of you that you desire?

Chapter Eight

Conclusion

LIFE AFTER ABUSE IS a daunting balancing act. You have to consider so many areas of your life and navigate relationships with others. This book is not meant to be the end-all to managing life after abuse. It's a guide with tools to support you on your journey. It's a way to note the areas you may forget or neglect as you move towards liberation and peace, particularly in terms of your un/learning, actualization, and centering.

Sometimes, you'll find that after a situation, you may need to refocus on an area that you previously handled. For instance, while writing the end of this book, I was in the middle of a break-up after several years. It was heartbreaking. I found myself going back to self-trust and self-love. I had to remind myself that I can trust that I gave my all in the relationship and that I can still love the parts of me that were hurt and sad.

As you plan for, or are currently in, your life-after-abuse phase, remember to prioritize your safety. Your home must be safe for you and those you care for. Are your windows secure? Have you changed the locks? Walk through your space and think about the ways you can feel safer. If you have children, consider having them do the same from their perspective. At work, if possible, speak with your manager or human resources about their domestic violence workplace policy. Schools are intentional about creating a safe environment, and making them aware of possible safety concerns allows them to ensure your children are well taken care of. While technology can be a benefit to our lives, make sure you take the necessary precautions, such as changing passwords, using different names, or turning off location sharing. Remember: you deserve to be safe in every area of your life.

One day, years ago, I met with a financial advisor. He worked at the bank that my employer used. We sat down and discussed my financial situation. I will never forget what he told me. "You are taking the steps, but the reality is...you need to make more money." He was right; I just wasn't making enough. The truth is, we can not save our way out of poverty. Most times, it's not a matter of budgeting or reckless spending; it's simply a matter of not having enough money. It's not simple, but it's true. I think we should discuss finances more. Please see the bonus chapter written by Nadia Vanderhall. I hope it helps.

Ultimately, we found ourselves in these unhealthy relationships because we are seeking love. It's human to want to be in a close partnership with someone. We desire loving relationships with our partners, family, and friends. We don't have to accept the falsehoods that we are unworthy of love or that love doesn't exist. We can reclaim something else. We can cultivate different values that align with our authentic selves. And that's the thing, we have to get back to ourselves. Who we are and the values we hold are vital to how we show up for ourselves and those we care about. These experiences with unloving, unhealed, abusive partners do not define us and don't have to be a part of our future.

Family is often our first teacher. Ideally, they show us how the world works, and that includes relationships. It may be the case that for many of us, our families don't always have the tools to teach us how to... It is our responsibility to learn what we need to pass down to others. As we get older and navigate life, we may come to realize that not only blood ties make a family. We can build something with new people and develop more profound and meaningful connections at all stages of our lives. Life after abuse does not mean leaving an intimate relationship that was abusive to continue accepting abuse from family.

Our new family can be filled with friends. Sometimes we meet people with whom we immediately connect. Other times, our friendships have run their course. It's up to you to decide. Consider what you need in a friendship, but also note when your symptoms of trauma are showing up, and you may need to self-regulate or take a step back. Friendships evolve and require care, just like any other relationship. If you are someone who needs your friends to check on you frequently, it may not be a good idea to have a close friendship with someone who calls once a year. Communication is crucial here. Be in community with your friends, ask for and share what's important to you and what's needed. Reciprocate. Initially, you may feel more needy. That's normal. Lastly, you don't have to share your experience with anyone. Your story belongs to you. Your experience is yours. All that you have experienced is yours. A caring friend will understand and respect that.

I can't reiterate enough just how important it is to focus on your SELF after an abusive relationship. It can be tempting not to worry about yourself or skip the hard parts, but that will only lead to potentially repeating behaviors you desire to let go of. There are facets of our culture that tell us to move and be productive, to go, go, go without looking back or pausing. Capitalism. Status. All the things that drive these systems of gender-based violence and partner abuse. Do not listen to them!

After the relationship, I want you to get to a space of re·SELF·tion. Fight for it! Re·SELF·tion is the state, act, and process of the restoration of self after experiencing relationship abuse. You can restore yourself by focusing on self-love, self-control, self-worth, self-discovery, compassion, and trust. How will you love and control yourself in this next phase of your life? What are you worthy of? What's new to discover? How will you show yourself compassion? How will you trust yourself again? As I mentioned in that chapter, this is the hardest but the most rewarding. I'm confident you can achieve **re·SELF·tion**. I believe in you and the power you have to save yourself.

I don't know you, but I am cheering for you. I am visualizing your healing. I am praying for your safety. I also know that you are enough and deserve all the types of love you desire. While your experience with abuse has changed you, it does not define you. It is your past, not your present, and has no place in your future. Survivors are amazing people. We have overcome experiences that could have literally killed us. But here we are surviving, achieving, and thriving. And, we did this because no one was coming to save us.

We saved ourselves!

Chapter Nine

Bonus Chapter

Nadia Vanderhall of Brands and Bands, LLC

DISCLAIMER: THE FINANCIAL ADVICE and information shared here are for educational purposes only. Everyone's situation is different, so be sure to assess what works best for you. I'm not your financial advisor, lawyer, or therapist—just someone here to provide guidance and help you make informed decisions. If you need personalized advice, consider speaking with a professional who understands your specific circumstances.

Know Your Money, Know Yourself: Breaking Free and Building a New Financial Future

I remember sitting with a client who had no idea she was being financially abused until our conversation. She didn't know how much money her husband made. She was given an allowance—*from her own paycheck*—and had zero access to their financial planner. Every time she asked questions about money, she was met with gaslighting, avoidance, or straight-up hostility from her husband. That conversation was painful, but it was also powerful. Because once she saw what was happening, she knew she had to take control. And she did.

If you're in a situation where money is being used as a weapon—whether through control, secrecy, or manipulation—you are not alone. The good news? You can take steps to reclaim your financial power. Let's break this down into what you need to know, what you can do, and how to move forward on your own terms.

Years ago, during the pandemic, I worked with a brand to talk about investing for women. It was a group of 50 women, and it was their first time learning about investing. It was not only an eye-opener to how important investing was, but also a reminder of any trauma that had taken a toll on their confidence to invest. There are several statistics around how confidence can keep women from not only investing but learning about money, but it compounds when it's in an environment that is abusive in many ways. Financial abuse compounds a different type of interest, not only to your spirit but also to your stacks.

Understanding Your Money: What You Don't Know *Is* Hurting You

One of the first things to realize is that financial abuse is *real*, and it often flies under the radar. I've seen the social media posts where it's hidden under laughter, or folks just scroll past. If you're in a situation where you don't have access to bank accounts, can't make independent financial decisions, or feel like you have to ask permission to spend your own money, it's time to take a step back and assess. The notion of "you aren't alone" doesn't get loud until you are and have to refocus your relationship with money.

Your Launching Pad:

You're just starting out and trying to figure out your funds, so I wanted to give you not only some tips but also break it up into areas of your "wallet" that you need to help pivot from the pain to your purpose.

- **Check your accounts.** If you have online banking, log in and review transactions. If you don't have access, that's a red flag. Get another bank account outside of the one that you might have with your partner/ex-partner. Use another mailing address and email that they don't have access to. Redirect any funds you have from deposits to your new account. If you are scared to do so, change your deposit amounts in smaller increments to build as you build your plan gradually..

- **Pull your credit report.** Sites like AnnualCreditReport.com allow you to check for free. Look for any accounts you don't recognize. Also, start reporting anything that isn't yours (it's called identity theft) to help you get your credit score back up to move better.

- **Start tracking your income and expenses.** Even if you only have access to part of the household finances, knowing what comes in and goes out is key. You can't measure what you don't track. Even if you feel it isn't a lot, learning to manage what you have now will make your money management better when you have more. Track for roughly 2 weeks: how much you spend, where, what account, and how you felt spending.

Saving Money To Pivot: Build Your Escape Fund

If you're planning to leave—or even if you're just preparing for possibilities—you need your own money. A *high-yield savings account (HYSA)* is one of the best ways to start stacking up cash quietly and securely. HYSAs are one of my favorite accounts to recommend to people. They are savings accounts that allow you to save at a higher interest rate than a regular savings account.

How to Do It:

- **Open a HYSA in your name only.** Use an online bank that isn't linked to your joint accounts.

- **Save small but consistently.** Even $10-$50 a week adds up over time.

- **Use cash-back apps or side income to

funnel extra money into your account. Small streams of income can build your financial cushion.

How Your Environment Shapes Your Money Mindset

Let's talk about *financial trauma.* It's not just a buzzword, but a real connection to how you handle, earn, and grow your money. If you've been controlled financially for years, even making basic decisions like buying groceries on your own can feel overwhelming. It's not just about numbers—it's about *unlearning* the fear, shame, or guilt that's been placed on you around money. It can legit numb you, but we are going to take your power back by shifting your mind.

Steps to Reframe Your Money Mindset:
- **Acknowledge the trauma.** You didn't "fail" financially—this was done *to* you.

- **Give yourself grace.** Learning how to manage money independently is a process.

- **Seek support.** Therapy, financial coaching, or even money-focused books can help you rebuild confidence.

I'm BIG on journaling, and I open up my client sessions asking about their origin with money. Their Money Story - I want to give you some journal prompts to write down and build your relationship with money. Write them out and read them out loud because this will help you unlock not only how you *think* about money but also how you *feel* about it. You will begin to get to a root-cause analysis and unpack your experience holistically:

Reflection on Financial Trauma
- What messages about money did I grow up hearing? Were they positive or negative?

- Have I ever felt fear, guilt, or shame around spending or saving money? Where do I think that comes from?

- How has my past financial situation influenced my approach to handling money today?

Recognizing Financial Control

- Have I ever felt like I had to ask for permission to spend my own money? How did that make me feel?

- Have I ever been denied access to financial information in a relationship? How did that impact my confidence in money?

- In what ways have others influenced my financial decisions, positively or negatively?

Reframing Your Money Mindset

- What does financial freedom mean to me?

- What is one small step I can take to rebuild my confidence with money?

- How can I start making financial decisions that

align with *my* goals and values?

Moving Forward With Confidence

- What would my ideal financial future look like in five years?

- What is one financial habit I want to unlearn, and what is one I want to build?

- Who can I reach out to for financial guidance or emotional support during this journey?

These prompts can help guide reflection on how to unlearn harmful money beliefs and rebuild confidence.

Starting To Invest With Little Money

Compound interest is an interesting thing - it allows you to take some of your money and place it in the right position to increase your sum over time. Once you've got some breathing room, it's time to think about *growth*. You don't need thousands to start investing—just consistency and patience.

Where to Begin:

- **Look into robo-advisors** (such as Fidelity or Public Invest) that allow you to invest with as little as $10.

- **Commit and Create:** Look to see how much you can commit yourself to each paycheck to start paying your future self. Also, consider leveraging Exchange-Traded Funds (ETFs) like VTI and VOO in fractional shares (think pieces of stock for a set price - that same $10).

- **If your job offers a 401(k), contribute at least enough to get the company to match.** That's free money you don't want to leave on the table. Also, call your HR to speak with the platform's service folks to get a grip on making those funds within your retirement fund grow.

Budgeting For Your New Life

Your budget can feel like a pain, but learning how you spend and manage your expenses allows your budget to become a personalized plan. It's simply a plan for your money for the month. Your money should now work for *you*—not the other way around. Creating a budget isn't about restriction; it's about *freedom*.

How to Set Up a Fresh Budget:

- **Prioritize essentials first.** Rent, food, transportation, and healthcare.

- **Find Your Ratio:** You've likely heard about 50/30/20 or 70/20/10, but I always stress the importance of understanding the reality of your money more than the ratio itself. Zero-based budgeting allows you to do that. Zero-based budgeting (ZBB) is a method of budgeting where every dollar is assigned a specific job, and your income minus expenses equals zero by the end of the month.

- **Automate your savings.** Set up direct deposits to your HYSA and investment accounts.

- **Give yourself spending power.** Even if it's just $20 a week for coffee or fun, having control over your own money matters.

You Are in Control Now

Leaving a financially abusive situation is hard, but staying stuck in one is even harder. My client? She didn't just leave—she *thrived*. She learned how to manage her money, built her credit, and eventually bought her own home. That budget gave us a tussle, but that season working together taught us both a lot. That could be you, too.

You *deserve* to know your money. You *deserve* financial freedom. You get to not only envision what that freedom looks like, but you get to color a different picture (in and out of the lines) as you go along. One of my favorite quotes is, "Be firm in your intentions, but flexible in your implementation." You are learning, unlearning, and relearning yourself and your money. Give yourself grace, but also get *up* to *get to* become the better person you want to be. Step by step, you *will* get there. One decision, one dollar, one day at a time. I'm so proud of you!

Your Questions Answered

WHY DO I MISS *him?*
It is absolutely natural to miss the person you were in a relationship with, regardless of how it ended. The transformation occurs when you don't act on that feeling in a way that puts you back in harm's way. Sometimes, we also have to remind ourselves why we left in the first place or why we are happy it ended. Yes, you miss him, but you also remember all the pain he caused you.

Are there any real success stories of an abuser reforming and becoming a good person and reconciling with their partner?

There are stories, few but some. However, this is often the result of separation and intense work done by both parties. It is virtually impossible to reform in the same space where the harm was caused. Even as the survivor, you need to be away from the person who hurt you in order to heal.

Will he hurt her too?

Possibly. He also may not. That's not really your concern. I know it's easy to wonder and question if she's feeling the same pain, but ultimately, does that resolve your own? You may feel moved to warn her, but that may not change anything. The person he is with now can't be your focus. However, your focus should be on yourself. If you feel the desire to reach out to her, consider re-reading Chapter Five and the section on self-control. Let that guide you back to focusing on your healing journey.

Has anyone ever ended up back in an abusive relationship, but with a different partner?

It is very common to find yourself in back-to-back abusive relationships. That is one of the reasons I wrote this book, so that we can break the pattern. If we find ourselves in another abusive relationship, we have to take time to focus on our self-love and self-worth. Reflect on how you'd rather be treated.

Why can't I make him leave?

The foundation of relationship abuse is power and control. You can't make him leave because he doesn't want you to have the power to do so. He only wants the power. If you find yourself desiring for him to go and telling him to isn't working, you may have to get law enforcement involved.

How do I deal with loneliness?

It is natural to experience loneliness after any relationship, even one that was violent. One of the ways I recommend dealing with the loneliness is journaling about what you are experiencing. That allows you to get out of your head. Also, this time is an excellent opportunity to try new things. What are some new hobbies you've wanted to try or places you've wanted to visit? Make a list and check off each item as you complete it.

Why am I still triggered?

It is very normal to still be triggered by something that reminds you of your experience. Sometimes we're taken right back to the moment and it feels real. It takes time and awareness. If you are aware of your triggers overtime you can incorporate tools and techniques you've learned. If you find this happening try and take several deep breaths and slowly breathe out. Remind yourself that you are safe.

Where can I go for help?

The help you receive will depend on your needs but calling your local domestic violence hotline can help you get clarity and resources even long after you've experienced relationship abuse.

Was it really that bad?

I would ask myself the same thing. The answer is always yes. Whether it happened a few times or for years it was bad. No one deserves to feel any kind of pain in a relationship. Sometimes when we have distanced ourselves from the situation, we don't feel the same way. But the truth is that it was that bad and it could have gotten worse but you freed yourself.

Will I ever feel safe again?

First ask yourself, what do you need to feel safe. When you have an idea of that, put them into practice every day. Be sure to remind yourself that you deserve safety. If this person is still contacting you, reach out to your local domestic violence agency to see what is available to you.

How do I explain this to my kids?

This will really depend on the age of the kids, their relationship with the person and yourself, and where you are on your healing journey. There are therapists who can provide support in discussing this with your children.

How do I stop blaming myself?

Blaming yourself is a natural thought. This is where you want to practice self-compassion (see page: __).

Why doesn't anyone believe us?

I wish there were a simple answer to this question. Unfortunately, there is a lot of stigma and bias around domestic violence. Because it's such a complex issue, many people are unwilling to take the time to understand what survivors experience truly. Sometimes people don't believe us because they think it's our fault. Other times, they don't want to believe us because it means they will have to confront their own experiences with abuse, either as a child, a partner, or a perpetrator. Additionally, society tends to uphold toxic patriarchy, homophobia, transphobia, and misogyny. Some people simply lack the empathy required to believe survivors.

Ultimately, we need to surround ourselves with people who genuinely believe in us and support us. We must disregard those who don't. They are not worth our attention. I believe you!

Is it possible to date after domestic violence?

Absolutely! It won't be easy, and I always recommend taking time for yourself before jumping into another relationship. One thing I find very important is learning more about healthy relationships. Many of us have never witnessed or experienced a healthy relationship. Knowing what a healthy relationship entails gives us a solid foundation for recognizing green, yellow, and red flags.

I've heard incredible stories of survivors who experienced loving, healthy relationships after years of abuse. I've experienced it myself and am grateful.. I will note that when a relationship is healthy, it may shed light on areas you thought you had healed. The difference is that you can address them with your partner in a way that allows you to process them without ridicule and abuse. It's wonderful!

What does healing even look like?
The process of healing will look different to each of us. Sometimes its being alone and focusing on yourself and your children. Other times, it looks like being able to say the person's name without cringing or crying. Healing can look like wearing what you want to wear, dancing like no one is listening, going after that job you've always wanted, or just saying yes to things you would have previously said no or had to ask permission to do. Make healing your own.

How do I tell my story or do I have to?
You do not have to tell your story to anyone at any point of time. Your story is your own. If you chose to tell your story, you get to determine just how much of it you share. Also, if you do decide to share about

your experience, you can limit who hears it. Not every survivor desires to be a public speaker.

How do I rebuild my life?

You rebuild your life much like how you build a home. Start with the foundation. Your mental, emotional health and safety are the foundation. Consider each brick laid a moment for you to rebuild your life. Take your time. Much like homes, you'll need help and guidance. Ultimately, this is your life, you're in control now. Create the life you need, want, deserve, and desire.

Will my life get better?

Unequivocally, yes! Life after abuse is hard, but it will get better. I encourage you to create the life you desire, one step at a time. Give yourself compassion and grace. Incorporate journaling into your daily routine. If accessible, go to therapy. *No One's Coming to Save You* isn't just a one-time read. It is one that you can return to time and again. It takes work and commitment, but life after abuse is a beautiful thing!

Acknowledgements

My kiddo, thank you for always being just who you are: amazing, creative, funny, driven, and kind. All of your dreams will come true. My goodness, you're so dope! You are the son I wanted and needed. You make me a better human being. Everything I do is to create the life you deserve.

Alana Brown, thank you for agreeing to write the foreword. It is an honor to have you set the tone and amplify my intentions for this book. I wasn't sure if you would say yes when I asked, but I'm glad you did. Somatic-Based Trauma Therapist Tameka Whittlesey for providing expert insight in such a short period of time. I'm grateful.

My New York crew. Alana Benoit for offering to be my developmental editor when being my friend is just as much work. Adriana, your eye for detail is unmatched. I love how you can break down my convoluted thoughts and ideas. Madinah, for making time for all the tears, breakdowns, mommy talks, and celebrations, and for holding me accountable and reminding me of my power. Shean, because I can always count on you to humble me and remind me of just where I come from, and I will always need that. Our long walks and talks set the tone for my clarity sessions. Tamika, if I didn't have a friend like you, I would have been in prison a long time ago. Your calmness is everything. December, you laugh at the most awkward times, and you taught me how to be rational; I appreciate that.

My "Spicy Nice Crew," Christine, Enovia, and Jameka, thank you for all the support, ideas, brainstorming, subcontracting, and planning sessions. You all remind me just how much Black women need business besties. A special thank you to Enovia because I don't know if you've ever told me no. "Can you help with this event?" Yes. "Can you be a board member?" Yes.

Kristie, you are so many things to many people. I am grateful for your encouragement and willingness to be a friend, confidante, board member, supporter, counselor, co-conspirator, and all the things. You're badass!

Sarah, for being my mentor, coach, sponsor, and friend. Thank you for every introduction, coaching session, dinner meeting, and connection.

Jay, for keeping me in alignment with my future self and holding space for me when I couldn't.

My cousin Greg, because you have been an inspiration to me our entire adult lives. You poured into me even during my darkest moments, and truly, the reason why I am writing this book on the other side of the walls.

Last but definitely not least, my parents, Christine and Roger, for instilling in me a sense of power and ambition that only two street-smart hustlers from Harlem could do. I am not whole without y'all.

Resources

Safety

1. Sullivan, Cris M., et al. "Impact of the Domestic Violence Housing First Model on Survivors' Safety and Housing Stability: Six-Month Findings." *Journal of Family Violence* 37, no. 4 (2022): 533–45.

2. Center for American Progress. *Ensuring Domestic Violence Survivors' Safety*. Washington, DC: Center for American Progress, 2020.

3. Time Staff. "How Domestic Abusers Have Exploited Technology During the Pandemic." *Time Magazine*, February 2020.

4. Safety Net Project. "Technology Safety Plan: A Guide for Survivors and Advocates." Accessed July 30, 2025. https://www.techsafety.org/resources-survivors/technology-safety-plan.

5. National Coalition Against Domestic Violence. "What Is a Safety Plan?" Accessed July 30, 2025. https://www.thehotline.org/what-is-a-safety-plan/

Finances

1. The Brands and Bands. Accessed July 30, 2025. https://www.thebrandsandbands.com/.

2. Woods, Parris. *The Black Girl's Guide to Financial Freedom: Build Wealth, Retire Early, and Live the Life of Your Dreams*. September 2021.

3. Stanny, Barbara. *Overcoming Under Earning: A Five-Step Plan to a Richer Life*. New York: HarperBusiness.

4. Housel, Morgan. *The Psychology of Money: Timeless Lessons on Wealth, Greed, and Happiness*. Harriman House, 2020.

5. Rodgers, Rachel. *We Should All Be Millionaires: A Woman's Guide to Earning More, Building Wealth, and Gaining Economic Power*. New York: HarperCollins Leadership, 2021.

6. Scovel-Shinn, Florence. *The Game of Life and How to Play It*. New York: TarcherPerigee.

7. Postmus, Judy L., et al. "Economic Abuse as an Invisible Form of Domestic Violence: A Multicountry Review." *Journal of Interpersonal Violence*, published online 2020.

8. Surviving Economic Abuse. *Guide*. Accessed July 30, 2025. https://guide.survivingeconomicabuse.org/.

9. The Allstate Foundation. *Moving Ahead Workbook*. Accessed July 30, 2025. https://www.allstatecorporation.com/the-allst

ate-foundation/relationship-abuse.aspx.

10. National Network to End Domestic Violence. *Financial Abuse Toolkit*. Accessed July 30, 2025. https://nnedv.org/resources-library/financial-abuse-toolkit/.

11. Mill, Alfred. *Personal Finance 101: A Crash Course in Managing Your Money*. Adams Media.

12. Twist, Lynne. *The Soul of Money: Transforming Your Relationship with Money and Life*. New York: W.W. Norton & Company.

Family

1. Tawwab, Nedra Glover. *Set Boundaries, Find Peace: A Guide to Reclaiming Yourself*. New York: TarcherPerigee, 2021.

2. Tawwab, Nedra Glover. *Drama Free: A Guide to Managing Unhealthy Family Relationships*. New York: TarcherPerigee, 2023.

3. Bellotti, Elisa, Susanne Boethius, Malin Åkerström, and Margareta Hydén. "Ambivalent and Consistent Relationships: The Role of Personal Networks in Cases of Domestic Violence." *arXiv* preprint, November 2021.

4. Richards, Akilah S. *Raising Free People: Unschooling as Liberation and Healing Work*. Akilah S. Richards, 2020.

5. Tsabary, Shefali. *The Conscious Parent: Transforming Ourselves, Empowering Our Children*. Namaste Publishing, 2010.

6. Carlisle, JC and Carla A. *My Epic Flow*. 2020.

7. Dunckley, Victoria L. *Reset Your Child's Brain*. New York: New World Library, 2015.

8. Jensen, Frances E., with Amy Ellis Nutt. *The Teenage Brain: A Neuroscientist's Survival Guide to Raising Adolescents and Young Adults*. New York: Harper, 2015.

Friendship

1. Break the Silence DV. "How to Comfort a Friend Who May Be in an Abusive Relationship." *Break the Silence DV Blog*, March 28, 2025. https://breakthesilencedv.org/how-to-comfort-a-friend-who-may-be-in-an-abusive-relationship/.

2. Sorrell, Deidra A. *The Black Friendship Project: A Modern Guide to Healthy Friendships*. December 2024.

3. Coleman, Chrisena. *Just Between Girlfriends: African-American Women Celebrate Friendship*. New York: One World/Ballantine Books, 1998.

4. Sow, Aminatou, and Ann Friedman. *Big Friendship: How We Keep Each Other Close*. New York: Simon & Schuster, 2021.

Self

1. Parris, Anana Johari Harris. *Self Care Matters: A Revolutionary's Approach*. Self-published, 2016.

2. hooks, bell. *All About Love: New Visions*. New York: William Morrow Paperbacks, 2018.

3. hooks, bell. *The Will to Change: Men, Masculinity, and Love*. New York: Atria Books, 2004.

4. hooks, bell. *Rock My Soul: Black People and Self-Esteem*. New York: Atria Books, 2004.

5. Renee, Nia. *Letters to You*. Self-published, 2020.

6. Coombs, Namaine. *Unleash Intentional Success*. 2022.

7. Steps to Hope. "Self-Compassion for Abuse Survivors." *Steps to Hope Blog*, May 5, 2025. https://www.stepstohope.org/blog/self-compassion-for-abuse-survivors.

8. Psychology Today. "Self-Compassion: A Must

for Survivors of Intimate Partner Abuse." *Psychology Today*, March 5, 2024. https://www.psychologytoday.com/us/blog/mind-games/202402/self-compassion-a-must-for-survivors-of-intimate-partner-abuse.

9. Break the Silence DV. "The Transformative Power of Self-Compassion and Self-Care: A Journey to Healing." *Break the Silence DV Blog*. https://breakthesilencedv.org/the-transformative-power-of-self-compassion-and-self-care-a-journey-to-healing/.

10. Bean, Lexie. "How Writing Letters to My Body Helps Me Heal from Sexual Assault." *them.*, April 13, 2018. https://www.them.us/story/writing-through-trauma-sexual-assault.

11. Perry, Bruce D., and Oprah Winfrey. *What Happened to You?: Conversations on Trauma, Resilience, and Healing*. New York: Flatiron Books, 2021.

12. Brown, Shanita, Dr. *Healing & Thriving After Domestic Violence: A Practical Guide for Black Women.* June 2025.

13. Moore-Lobban, Shavonne J., PhD, and Robyn L. Gobin, PhD. *The Black Woman's Guide to Overcoming Domestic Violence: Tools to Move Beyond Trauma, Reclaim Freedom, and Create the Life You Deserve.* Oakland: New Harbinger Publications, 2022.

14. Gross, Melody. *Reclaim Your Resilience: A Guided Journal for Survivors.* 2021.

About the author

Melody Gross is a bold voice, trusted expert, self-proclaimed disruptor, and unwavering advocate for survivors of domestic violence.

Born and raised in Harlem, Melody writes nonfiction that challenges, affirms, and educates. Her work doesn't shy away from the uncomfortable—it leans in with honesty, clarity, and a deep belief in the power of truth. As a survivor herself, she brings both personal insight and professional expertise to the page and speaking engagements, bridging the gap between what survivors actually need and what the world too often fails to provide.

Melody's journey to becoming a speaker and author was born out of necessity. Speaking out saved her, and now, she writes to create pathways for others to feel seen, heard, and supported. Whether she's consulting and training companies through her business Couragoeus SHIFT, leading prevention work through her nonprofit, the Eva Lee Parker Foundation, or mentoring those navigating harm, Melody's message is clear: we all have a role to play in ending intimate partner violence. Her books *No One's Coming to Save You* and *You Can't Save Us* are urgent, raw, and an invitation to listen deeply, act bravely, and remember that healing is possible, even when it's hard.

She now resides in Charlotte, North Carolina, with her talented and funny teenage son. Away from the page and podium, Melody finds joy in decorating her home for Christmas, randomly dancing, singing, or spitting rap lyrics, and exploring all forms that celebrate art, culture, and history. Her life and writing are a testament to resilience—not the polished kind, but the type forged in fire, rooted in community, lit by optimism, and driven by courage.

www.ingramcontent.com/pod-product-compliance
Lightning Source LLC
Chambersburg PA
CBHW052029030426
42337CB00027B/4926